epicormic

Also by Nicola Bowery

Bloodwood (Bunda Press, 1996)
Goatfish (Bunda Press, 2007)
married to this ground (Walleah Press, 2014)
child in the wings (Walleah Press, 2019)

Walleah Press
South Launceston
Tasmania, Australia 7249

www.walleahpress.com.au
ralph-walleahpress@proton.me

Cover design by Casey Schuurman

Cover photos by Nicola Bowery (eucalypt bark and epicormic)
Set in Perpetua 12.5/15 by Ralph Wessman
Printed by IngramSpark, Melbourne

ISBN: 978-1-764120-03-6

epi cor mic

new & selected poems

nicola bowery

CONTENTS

from **married to this ground**   2014

from **child in the wings**   2019

To Harry

epicormic

new poems

in the wake of

in the wake of fire

there's a rhythm to waiting

like the seed waiting below charcoal and ash
waiting to burst in a frenzy
knows what it must do

and how it resists   delays
for whatever reason

waits

the charred tree waiting

I am knocking on your door
and my knuckles are blackening

the soot embedded in your hide
still shedding

hide   animal word   not yours

but then   savagely burnt
what are you?

the forest is silent

and then this other waiting

barely a chink of time
between the first rain settling ash
and the first pandemic gasp
barely a month of days

a microbe announces itself in the ether
beyond seed   seedless
but proliferating itself unfathomably
a corona unattached to the moon

multiplying   disseminating infinitely

announces un-ease

dis-ease

teasing

the silence fire had left in its wake
and the foment of this new mystery
collided

the years stretched to three
but let's say two
two years were a collision
a collusion of waiting

in the wake of
what is woken? what wakes?

(time is awake in a different rhythm)

you might say to time
what and how?

and time would answer
momentary bells

rain comes
so long longed for
but longing once sated becomes
invisible
washed away beyond mention

and then this other waiting

all the babble
the human speech uttered as a groping
knowing so little

and the forest's silence
the forest not uttering
not words

that eye asleep in the black chant rhythm of the burnt
the burnt
how this eye can't detect but suddenly
a nodule swells

the epicormic bud
pops

how long it's been sleeping
a closed eyelet in the bark

then a spout of green
or a scarlet shoot
out of the black straitjacket
fire's gift   its first bouquet
the very first promise of future

(time is awake in a different rhythm)

first on the scene
green gathers its brushes
dabs tiny dots and squiggles
green the colour of ordinary
and now the pivot

who is painting?

bud-bursts spaced on the black trunks like toe holds
feet gripping the black bark
sure-footed
scaling the ladder into the future
a leafy delicate flurry around the foot
full of green hope   effulgence
essentially familiar
as green is

trees listening
but how do we know?
each of us owning our particular conversations
with the arboreal
possessing   pirating
saying we have the language
blathering our human speech at their silence
reliant on their standing
the tall perpetuity of them
their heroic stance
having borne so much wounding

let them talk amongst themselves
if indeed they do
let their own *ouch*-crying be their own
let the epicormic posy be the poultice
offer soothing

I shall keep looking   watching

the onto of eyes
look onto and upon
look out and onto

a love story?

but let's not be sentimental
this is a fierce pact
let's call it out

a desperate ruthless infatuation
to the possible death
to the possible life

the seed beneath bark
or the seed in its hard casing
scattered on ground

hankering for fire

a necessary dalliance with the arc of time
seed hankering for fire

a necessary infatuation

the language of wounding is my language
not the tree's

that moment in time
when drought and heat   wind and storm
play their deft hands

when too many leaves are yelping yellow
falling like parched petals

call it longing?

and what answers?

an arrow of dry lightning
the chink of glass   spark from a wire   a tool?

wind whipping in as cohort   sympathiser
true go-between   fanning the drama

a passion of flame and seed
years and years in the waiting

but oh the cost
the unbelievable odds   the gamble

from my edge   the cleared lands behind me
part of me there   part of me leaning into the forest

like peering through hospital glass to the injured
the glass blackly smeared

what's left of the trees hardest hit
bare arms reaching up

twig fingers gesticulating   a desperate sign language
to what to whom?   a deaf sky busy with clouds?

and at ground level a sort of skirt around each tree
a black skirt of bare ground
where the new shoots of bracken hesitate

you burned hot there

a sort of hush   a deference

don't dare say the wreckage-scape has its own
stark beauty   don't say that

but look at the sudden white fungus
shelfing out from the black trunk

and a small bird perched
must be phantom   no small birds yet

the timidity of my gaze
who knows anything of the other

each in our separate orbits

tree sap rising unintelligible to our ears
the closed vessel   sap rising sap seeping
how dare pry into that secret
no   peel nothing back   I won't prod you
or pry into and under your black armour
with my own faltering gestures
lungs perhaps that I foist on you
to do my breathing

can I help you at all after your immolation
anything concrete
any shopping?
can I fan those bouquets you are holding
is it wearying to carry so many?
tell me something
even though your leaf messenger is feeble
fragile
a tentative emissary

I am knocking on your door
my knuckles are still blackening

addressing you   forest
my eyes pushing past your black exclamations
I can overload you with verbiage
word-garbage

but you startle and stupefy with your
rigid uprightness as if nothing
nothing will daunt you

this forbearance   endurance
is terrifying

you compel me to ogle

tenderness

I offer that but your back is turned

tree talk

they say the tree says
they say trees speak to each other
the tree feels
they feel for each other

the puny projection onto the twig
one's own vulnerable tendrils

you could say there was a burning
and then   (collapse time)
an effusion of covered faces (pandemic)
that had nothing to do with burning
(collapse time)

when the masks came out
long after the flames

(collapse time)

when the don't knowing had reached its zenith
and as if to bandage our ignorance
we muffled ourselves further
bandaged our mouths

and by then
green was dominant again

asserting itself   rampant
refused to join that waiting room

splashed itself over the charcoal
drummed on the black shiny bark
strummed   strummed the future

sooty black and green
sooty black and green

what the flames had whistled over
what the rain polished
what the green sprang from

finally the tinkle of a small bird
(I've been waiting)

night rain so deliciously soft
like a swooshing of silk or taffeta
when some things have been hard

the sharp detail of night sounds
and bulky bulbous shapes in watery moonlight
the forest's wounds hidden

a strange liberating rapture
amidst the insoluble
the world's public and private sufferings
torments   irreversible injustices

the rain soft and embalming

the shadow of the burnt tree is remarkably pale
a pale jettison

viridian sedge tips proliferate
along with lomandra spears
extra brazen after the blazing

and the forest floor froths and surges
thrusts up seedlings   tree ferns   bracken   weeds
in a green frenzy

but the human world's engines are on low rev
the idling thing   on idle

we listen to our own
listlessness

the epicormic buds have slowed
a terrible latency hangs around them
as if echoing our lassitude

does the tree shrug its damaged shoulders?
mutter *get on with it*
get on with it

it's a time to whimper
whimper laments

I lament my boot sole buckled from hot ash back then
I lament the chocolate bark of the brown barrel gum
no longer being chocolate
I lament the forest's innocence being lost

but the stillness this morning
is an apology from the sky
a sorry   a soothing

delight in the tiny yellow-rumped thornbills arriving
first ones after fire
a sudden explosion of small-bird chatter

forget lament

out of the ash

came forth

bursaria

regrowing its thorns

inarticulate speech of the heart

ash as ground

dust to dust

find the heart there

resprout

after rain and rain
the sun beams out its hunger

melts the ice in the bird bowl this frosty morning

statuesque trunks in their waiting
the black armour that won't be shed

and back then
how could you guess that this bubble here
my writing space with its five cheeks of glass
would hold firm   inviolate

inconceivable that only one glass cheek
grumbled at the heat   cracked

back then

disbelief that smoke had a source and it was close

remember how I delivered your lunch

and I was out the gate fleeing as the wind changed

and new flames surged

aware it was a *close shave*

like all the words forever loaded

condolence   *for their loss   for their loss*

try not to think of the millions

scurrying or flitting between flaming tree trunks   roasted

for their loss   for their loss

I was stupidly worried for the smart car I'd borrowed

close shave

let's say words like *duck breast* and *peach*

remember

I delivered a peach and a smoked duck breast in a lunchbox

you were grateful if dazed

fire had taken you over

a horse neighs
how rarely a neigh arises

the black cockies maundering
masquerading as moaners

four eagles showing off their wheeling circles

the bigger birds have moved back in
but the ground-hopping ones are still scarce

and the leech is
nowhere

I peer into the forest   its collective knowledge
as if it's one being   one recovering patient

but there are characters   distinctions

how the manna gum with its flirtatious ribbons
has quickly shunned the sooty bandages

and how the tall mountain grey   *monkey gum*
flaunts its acrobatic upper branches
with a triumphant survivor's glee

while the brown barrel being the most populous
has born the brunt   holds its black robes close

weathers what comes

frisson
silky spooky word
that seizes me

the dead giant trees
ghosted grey
leave a huge wake

of frisson

obituaries have an in-built frisson

the owl's droppings
braided regurgitations
offer a faint frisson

and what the fox leaves
vestiges of offal
slightly more

you could say
the optimal amount of frisson is hard to organise

how close the dead branch lands

frisson

this continuity of rain
that stretches over the summer
as if still offering comfort

earth spilling   its letters liquid
structures collapsing with saturation
lichen iridescent on the garden chairs
the planet tilts with its sodden sleeves

our frogs having the time of their life
vociferously applauding the deluge
gurgles and gutturals
plops

how do the trees still stand with their roots swimming?
all the loosening   but the tall spines are resolute
holding to attention in a stark phalanx
with their black sheath-coats and green furs
necklaces   rings of green flurry

nothing flakes
the tree must not whimper itself out in flakes
must not whimper

but there are signs
signs of the black bark splitting vertically
as if the tree is preparing to shed the casing
to break out from the straitjacket
as if coaxed by the bud-budding attendants
as if here and there the rigour can be softened

birds quickening the air
with their wing-eddies

just now
a convoy of choughs in flight
their satin backs echoing charcoal
and their cream-white underwings
the sunlit flashes on the upper branches

in the glade
a thicket of regrowth
thickened after fire
saplings like teenagers on a street corner
gathering

a sort of conversation cluster
of the next tree generation
animate voices
dense with promise

the butcherbird this morning flagrantly cheerful
so sure of himself and this one such a songster
bright and clear   optimistic as an angel

but maybe he's just decimated a fledgling
gorged himself
his cruelty and lyricism pivoting on the barbed wire

you notice the first forest geebung flowering since the fire
and a kingfisher taunts with his insistent piping
you can't see me   taunts his invisible beauty

also unseen
the subterranean promise of fungi

and there's a quoll sighted   dashing across the road
another survivor

green has fulfilled its softer messaging
pampering the wounded
how much was needed
how much moist bandaging swathing cosseting
the green swaddling
and rain's constant medicine

the word lull comes in

then the rain stops as if there's been enough weeping
jets write again on the sky
and in the slow pulse of covid time
the plague is waning

something is telling us
get back into your dry boots
hear their tough soles rasp on gravel
hear that brittle rustle in the new leaf litter

go back to the dry the raucous the wanting

a tree is singing to itself
shuffling a note out of its charred corset

you can hear the faintest whisper
of messages between absent leaves

some epicormic posies   their task completed
are now shrivelling
the ladder steps discarded

the black covers of the bark book
starting to be shed

to show what's underneath

and likewise we drop our masks
dare to sing

in the wake of
in the wakc of firc

covid time

strange time   covid time   yet (extra) ordinary
a heightened habitation with ordinary

chairs swallowing our interior selves
all the ordinary objects   plates   spoons   the bed
shouting along with us *what is freedom?*

when science was hidden away with hope
and *don't know don't know* that first year

and we were addled by the covid riddle
subtracted and excised (sure we exercised daily)

each of us with our pot plant flowers of fear
torpor   inertia   we tended them
tenderly

compared their bonsai growth with our permitted
playmates we weren't allowed to touch

so we touched ourselves
seeking reassurance

**cancellation became a slinky seductive way
of living**

the *un* the *un* the *non*
expanding like a fungal network

the highway lost its bristling direction
we fantasised the world stopping
the planet resuscitating   cleansing its lungs
untrampled

but joggers proliferated
and dogs and dogs and dog shit
the grass of lawns and parks crumpled and moaned

the sea we couldn't reach was no doubt still advancing
waving its arms upward   rising   sea-rising

as *gabble gabble* told us how to live on a leash
to breathe without air

wash your hands wash your hands

happy birthday to me

collapse time

call it plague   revert to medieval   and manacles

(time was asleep in a different rhythm)

the air with its load of microbes
blooming around the globe
such a Promethean shackling of the world
to that not–mountain   its tethers   invisible chains
corona such a pretty word

pontifications   oracular utterances
military language as in fire battling
and epidemiologists the new gods
leaping into the screen-glare
steering us through the narrow channels   the whirlpools
all knowing   unless they confessed to *don't know*
where we all huddled
what appalling ineptitude we all shrieked

the virus a sickle sweeping under

that first year of riddling time

remember how the surface was suspect
how it might attack with its mantle of microbes
that great uprising of fear   remember that?

and touch-free deliveries and car boots
the tiny spray bottle boasting 99.9%
consider   in that time   strange time
our slaughter of companionable germs
our attack on the vibrant the symbiotic
the cosy company of dustmites
precious co-travellers
could I hear them pleading *save us save us?*

we didn't question our savage supremacy
our tottering hierarchy
we kept on anaesthetising our penumbras
but by then we were all handless maidens
our hands washed away   flesh dissolved in alcohol
and no one was hearing such whispers
they belonged to our conversations with ourselves
touching ourselves again
handless   always safer

at the masked ball of corona

we were all masquerading   hooked on the mask
the mask hooked on

landscape of the face disrupted   lips hidden
grins grimaces gasps   shushed

the eyes as messengers
could we trust them?

the mask a sort of monk
encouraging silence

M for muffle   mute   mask   monk

tagged and tracked and blipped

a frenzy of QR codes pinging on someone's screen

language losing its buds and flowers

a deity of digits   the staccato hammering of numbers
in the guise of clarity   inducing an hypnotic haze

a shock a numbing   a numinous quality in the slipstream
numbers as arrows pretending to be sharp
blunting   avoiding the heart   a false fodder

43   692   8   4597621   0

language losing its buds

**and along with all that was invisible
in the ether**

the alien microbes and the flowering fear
the torpor and lassitude and bafflement
there was subservience and infantile obedience
and a sort of collectivism   the community of screen
and *zoom* which defied the magnified solitude
and the death musings one held under one's skin
the future collapsing in on itself   becoming phantom
and there were wonders of resilience and patience
and service and compassion
along with suspicion and protestations
paranoia and anguish and tell-tale coveting
that time was all these things swirling
in the once benevolent air
turned demonic

tipped into May windblasted

as though the world's distress and unsettling needed
a hefty wind for May's announcements
unusual for May

    anticippointment   the certainty of uncertainty
    the certain constraint of two arms' length
    the uncertain reach of the masked breath

      the word *boulangerie* comes in
      a comforting lyrical word

      dream on

consider the disparities

here the forest vitally burgeoning again
as we humans wilted   wallowed

elsewhere grisly images   open graves
death creeping closer
the helpless language of condolence
for their loss   for their loss

hospital images   heroes
regalia of pandemic   blue robes   perspex armour
faceguards thrusting as if to vanquish air
that hazardous concourse

elsewhere locks on tower blocks

and here the trees impervious
(I'm sure of that)

never was the distinction between species
so sharp   the trees impervious   the roos

and the human tremulous

in the small circles of covid time

the house   the two of us within it   unmasked

M for mulling and muddling and the mountain of it
for mirror
the mirror and mystery of marriage
the mirage   the matter

we talk of how to live   of definitions
life is suffering
life has suffering
you prefer *life is unsatisfactory*
but I say my ground is joyful
that suffering can bang on the window
and sometimes shatter it
but the ground remains as ground

you report two peregrines and a hobby this morning
with the hobby chasing a peregrine
which suggests nesting   hope there   restoration

and free flying

evening mopokes   up to three at times
the tawny frogmouth's metronomic incantation

beating time

almost too faint the heartbeat of the human world

retreating under each individual skin
the solitary workouts

and the gym-junkies glimpsed through windows
stompers on treadmills
the furious thrashing and bullying of muscles
private tyrannies of exercise and fear
making sure the blood is beating

while the tree in the street
trapped in its bitumen anklet
tried perhaps to remember its roots

how brief it might seem in the future this interlude
this illusion of stopping

we had nothing to complain of

choose your special friend
like kindergarten
buy your play lunch
and meet by the creek
abandon your mask to the grass
crawl in to the coffee cup
the perfected design of the cake-box
crawl in there
      all is well

all manner of things
the platypus appeared on the dot to greet us
sidled his shiny back out of the shaded water
it wasn't about eyes meeting
purely the sleek of his back
his ripple
      all was well

our repetitions coddled and soothed us

a roo in the rain licking his forearms
as the rain kept wetting them

repetition of the same view
but the clouds ever changing
repetition of the same walk
and the morning crisp or sodden

my familiars   the swamp wallaby   grass
twigs in the groundcover
the manna gum on the east

the insistent note of the mudwasp
busying on the window frame

yet as science assumed hope and power

and we were injected   and again injected
there was no free flying and our cocoons stifled us

and there was a strange guilt around this impatience
given our comfort

the self was ashamed to be individual
the global was dominant   the hauntings
the inequities of suffering

it was all so much larger than oneself
the sinister stealth speeding up whichever mutant
the toxic vapour

it seemed treacherous to relish spaciousness
in that wider anguished world

the *I* needed to be erased

again injected and injected   protected

there was an easing of the rules

and even so the day had rigid truths
and deprivations

out to lunch
the large crumb clinging to the man's beard
finally decided to drop
as he talked and talked

perhaps he was too hungry
and we had become too used to silence

how vast is the distance between selves
how savagely vast

while the trees back here
announced a possible language

finally it all reverted to the ordinary

the ordinary that was no longer *extra* ordinary

we had all been so hushed and muffled and awed
and somehow blanketed
and needed to become noisy again
to celebrate our mouths

for sure   inertia had its own wake   lingered
forgotten selves needed reawakening   trusting the air
the usual markers of jet trails   highways   gridlock
crept back into their places
our death musings receded
we appeared confident   we had emerged

remember that Berlang picnic on the river?
like a sudden glimpse of a forgotten paradise
not a mask in sight and all these people
like a big painting   *déjeuner sur l'herbe*
the revelation of laughing faces
mouths

we had emerged

from

Bloodwood

1996

Jackeroo country

She slips from the table,
that lasso of voices. Cuts loose.

She fetches her jackeroo's wand
the whip that she's whittled

to speak her tongue.
Caresses the stick

grooved for the grip
runs the lash of rope

along her thumb
a blessing of spit

on the hide at the tip.
She lifts her arms, poised to speak.

The country turns brown
there's dust in her teeth

she's way past the border
hills on their backs

acres and acres roll out unmapped
her horse in the kiss

of her knees.
FLICK!

The earth's ribs crack.

She has spoken.

Dead nun

Flattened crow, wheeled out
like a lesson in arithmetic.
Death, minus one,
taught by a pickled nun.

I'm not ready for instruction.
Spiders stiffen quietly in corners,
an ant kisses the sand.
I am as virgin of death as they come.

Mother Agatha is dead.
Hurry girls, form a line.
I don't want to. She'll smell.
Move on, move on!
You're not at death's door yet.

She wasn't a person, not even a beetle.
Kept in the back room to wither in secret
then served up on a trolley after homework.
She's gone to Jesus. Say goodbye.
I don't want to say goodbye.

The line is moving at the pace of one peep only,
the chapel suffocates in chrysanthemums.
There's a faint whiff of fish,
the smug stare of too many candles,
the sputter of a giggle about to burst.

She's very neat in her tight-fitting box,
a cardboard cut-out, black feathered still,
her tiny paper hands folded in a holy posture.
She looks beyond the fuss of genuflection.
What about her bridal gown, her smile for Jesus,
the hole her soul escaped from?

I want to jab her toe
and ask her where she's going
but my knees are melting.
I want to be horizontal and carted away.
There are too many candles in Heaven.

Hush girls, off to bed.

Joan

Her house is the hot-blooded one.
The red bricks throb, a pulse of rum.
Plaster peels a rainbow bruise
a flip-flap door lets the tom-cats cruise —
windows come and go like black eyes.

Her fire burns bright with the picket fence.
I'm hired to teach her mother-sense
yet her brood is six and mine is one
her lap is vast, my knees are trim —
her heart's an ample cove for flotsam.

Screams at dawn. She knows I know.
I hover and snoop like a fly
tweaking her compost. She offers me gloves
but her floors are fresh as lavender sea —
the flyscreen tangles in the one plum tree.

She knows I know she boots all the rules.
Her chickens peck free, her skirts are their school.
She laughs at her luck, offers me tea
my lips filter the germs in the crack
my heart's an udder shrivelled black —
we laugh because she knows.

Desert

I'd thought only of stone —

a pock-faced hulk
    tongued by snakes

a landlord sun
    with skulls for rent

yet here I am held
    in the fur of an oak

hammocked in wind
    as gentle as floss

a butcherbird feeds me
    twigs of worm

a dingo woos
    a midday love

and bloodwood bends
    to drop me apples

I grin into space
    like a camel on heat —

I'd thought only of stone.

Eastern Papua

It was the first birth I'd witnessed
and I was agog with the miracle
from the moment the boy banged on the nurse's door
and we ran through the tropical moon-blaze,
the mission crotons gaudy even in moonlight,
my skin zinging with that other miracle –
the first breath from the sea.
So this child had chosen wisely
when to enter the gate.

We ran to the tin room, the labour ward,
the woman squatting in the doorframe
the iron-legged bed
and atop the scratched cupboard
the one other witness
Mother of all mothers
two hands high plaster of Paris
with her turned head.

The nurse was scooping the last performing mother
off the rubber pad – a tabby with her clutch –
and the woman half-giggled at the joke
before she moaned
and we coaxed her to the bed.
It wasn't her first
her body knew its work
she worked quietly
and so soon – the disc of hair.

Our gasps — the neck was noosed!
Four hands pulled, eased the knot
and there was the honeybrown fruit
glistening, not a blemish.
Then the dark-maroon haversack,
a few daubs of scarlet.

Clamping the new one to her rib
the woman swung her legs down,
the boy and a man reclaimed her
her eyes uttered thanks
and they all made off into the moon's hands.

Seven days in a croft

1

I take the coldest room.
The window frames the cautious daffodils
and beyond, juniper, spruce, moor.
First knots of larch in the tweed
burn-stains of heather scorched for grouse
musk-breathing birches
linen snow on the far-flung ridge
my fingers stuttering in mittens.

2

The gander stabs the ground for seed
badgers his bride
cranks the frost in his gullet
honks out bells.

3

We play crofter and wife
you bake the bread
a glamour loaf and I stitch cloth.
We scavenge in the crisp snow
of the bed.

4

Wide, wide the moor's pelt.
The snow hare killed on the road
before his colour turned. We do the turning
ochre-green, vermilion, rouge

as the sun cajoles us up the burn
blinks, is gone
to lurch us violet-clad in dusk.

5

Flung out of the shed
the lamb's first clutch on the field is fraught.
Larch buds are fraying.
My mittens itch in the moulting wind.

6

As the sun declares itself, noon-bold,
you ditch your coat behind the rowan.
Forearms rolled, you declare
the mountains are your match
they bow at your boots, call you lover.

Witch-wise in my burlap caul,
I wait to thaw myself by the moon.
Sunset-moonrise I am finally ripe –
I throw my cape, bask in the salmon silver light.

7

The true crofting man counts no hours.
As the moon inflates
he saddles Fergus, his highland dun
and trots uphill to ride out the night.

In the morning I can't see hooves returning
but his wife's out there
humping turnips.

Turning grey

It's time to dig for silver
time to bare my silver root
No!   call it plain
grey   grey   grey as rain
slag on the step
a sea of slops   insipid foam
mould on the yoghurt dip
grey as the colour of groan.

My mother
she grannied me young
grey   grey   grey
she was grey before her time
and now her crime comes down to me
I must declare it
rip the veil of bottled stain
the gaudy wig
and find the white-wicked flame.

Hair is the woman's crown
hair is the sword of the nun
hair outlives the skin
hair is the goddess-wand
soul flambé   the pillow love
the fluted mane for man
to twine his fingers in
a flower to perm and plume
and primp to a stupid shine —
I am grey before my time.

Yesterday I found my mother
in her prime
smiling a passport grin
like a silver doyenne
beautiful.

And today there's an epidemic!
Young girls white to the gills
pop out of carparks
maiden fern shrivels in a grey faint
the lake is filmed with asbestos
frogs are leaping in gabardine
an angel punk sprouts antennae
from her steel-grey cabinet of skull
babies birth grey
wizened out of past lives.

I plant bluebells in my ears
but oyster fur is barnacling
my weathered rock and all my fears
are frothing in a cloudburst of snow.

I am grey before my time.

Portuguese millipede

Nothing will eat him
hence his graffiti will multiply.
What he writes is indecipherable
yet we fear it must be a poison letter
it must be the last word.
Why else would he stow away
over the sea
and haul his cylinders of cyanide
over the hill
and bury himself days and months
in his black satin cummerbunds
underground
sharpening his pen
until drunk on the sodden earth
some memory irritates him
a hot leaf
the sun on his back
and killjoy that he is
he climbs
neat as a funeral clerk
with his two fastidious feelers
spilling no ink
and his thousand hair-legs
impeccably rhymed
he climbs
and hangs on the white wall
an exclamation
but if you find him at his calligraphy
and poke *Hoy! Is that message for me?*
he snaps himself shut
into a full stop
his last word.

from **Conversation round a birth**

1

What the fates…!

I was digging for my voice
rummaging my body's rooms for sound

when you answered, faint
as if beyond the clouds you hollered

then, cloudborne
swooped.

Three days on
I heard your echo in my womb.

What was I to do
but throw my hands to the sky

laugh
laugh with my love

for love had written you
no question

you were not to be erased.

2

Clouds following
mystified by your descent
hang ponderous in the March sky

break their vows
plunder the sun-shot ground.

Worlds turn about
you swill in your amniotic dome
the mustard crust of the earth dissolves.

Amazed
we open our mouths
drink in the scent of seed

your fizzing egg
the flush of grass.

3

Imposter!
Impossible sprite

look what you've done
unstitched my life

pulled on the thread
and snagged your own umbilical worm.

You've ripped my map
your foetal winch is grinding me back

I was this and this
and bound for there

I've incubated years to bloom.
Now this flower in my womb!

What woman must brew.
Oh I thought I'd borne what I was due.

Yet you lighten my spine.
Are you winged?

5

What if…what if…
A jot of blood!

Are you testing?

I lie still three days
like an old novel.

The lady is confined
to save her babe.

The doctor prods
I want him nowhere near your jewel.

Nobody asks me how I feel.

The pact with you comes clear
Fear!

Are you bailing out?
Abseiling off the wall?

Chicken!

I'm game
Are you?

6

Larva on the moon

a slice of you
a slice of moon

stitched on the scan
your colours gloomed

a silent blurred embroidery
as you whirl to decibels beyond our ken.

Dare I see you have a spine and shin?
How many centimetres bone?

Your hand, a tiny prong
upheld

waves
forgives our sacrilegious eye

as you jive between protoplasm and birth.

In your bobbing skull
the mystery of your will.

From my womb to the screen
you have leapt beyond me.

Moon-creature
I call you *he*.

7

Child, we've brought you west
following the umbilical thread
of the sea's edge, that nourishment.
The great mother emptying her breasts,
milk frothing at her thousand teats,
at the hem of her long blue skirt
and the beach guzzling like an infant.

The great mother, her vast amniotic pond.
I rock you, rock you in that balm
until the day's limpets, the fussing bee
and fly are hushed by the moon
and like the first creature delivered from the salt
ungainly, mute, I clamber onto land.

From the dark the sea mutters
like a mother soon to be scorned.

We head west to unmothered ground.

8

Where eagles hang their hooks
in the sky, plunge
unhook the rabbit's eye.

Nullarbor, where nothing holds.

Jilted back in time
my thread unwinds
I lose my hold on woman's ground.

Nullabor, where nothing holds.

Your heart gathering blood
as my heart spills. In this threadbare place,
the sea's lost bed.

Nullarbor, where nothing holds.

A litter of shells tells the old caress
but little else.
There's talk of the dead.

Nullarbor, where nothing holds.

The snake's black mouth.
A dingo yells.
My babe, I am losing hold.

Nullarbor, where nothing holds.

10

In this worry ward
women wait for birth,
high above the city's grid
holding their cracked eggs.

In the corridor
meek as a girl
I am waiting for a bed
whilst women pad about me
pushing their barrows of dread.

High above the city's grid
this incubation coop –
the windows barred with slatted lids
as if a hawk might swoop
out of the mid-winter blue
and snatch.

Women tread about me.
One wheels her body like a rented house.
When will the tenant move out?
Another drifts, airborne
dazed as a child by her balloon.

And three who lunge for the balcony door,
their spinnaker wombs billowing –
nurses jittering in their wake
'Nicotine…underweight…'

But the door shushes on its rubber fringe
and the women puff
into the blue mid-winter day
light as air.

11

I must give birth to death

I must give birth

to death
to death

This topsy-turvy loom
has woven death in my womb

Birth death
death birth

I must give death

birth

12

Are you Hermes?
Was this your trickery

to wind me back to the egg
dapple me with silver, speck me with lead?

When I peeped in the cul-de-sac
of my womb, you were gone.

Was this your trickery, Hermes?
To taunt me with silver, leave me with lead.

14

Death could not speak of itself.

It needed your ears
your half-winged toes
your elegant attenuated hands
the fingernails yet without their moons.
It needed your closed pregnant eyes
your lips
their exquisite poise of silent-speak.
At the base of the spine your rosette wound.

Death at the half-way point. Half-way
between the underworld of your dark-shut eye
and this, the winter sun
your bright unpolished skin
bursting into flame
as we feed you to the earth.

Your fingernails will gather dirt
not moons.
Nothing is sacred.

Death needed you to speak of this.

from

Goatfish

2007

The muster

(North Coast, Scotland)

The morning the rain stopped
the one crofting family across the strath*
the only one that had stayed with the sliding hills
came out of their honest grey croft
came out to muster their ten cows.
Three men and the woman in flapping skirt
danced jigs on the turf
they juggled their arms
their swearing bounced off the hill
the hill that was heaving as they danced
heaving its deck of heather and mud
and the beasts kept rolling slowly like boulders
unfussed by the hustling band
(there was no ramp or railing
no funnelling in any direction)
and after an hour or so
each figure still jigging on its own string
as if bobbing on water
(these men were used to boats)
the mustering was done, the act of it,
they all went in for a dram
and the boulders rolled into the hill.

* a river valley

Moods of Strathan
(North coast, Scotland)

The spick-white hull of the holiday croft
is too clean for the ancient hill
and its clearings —
too white and spruce for the muck
sluicing off the slope
in the daily scud of rain.
I hide in the whitewashed cell
nosed to the Arctic.
At my back the mountains Loyal and Hope
stay in their wraps.

Rain and sheep gnaw at the earth
gnaw at the cliff
gnaw the one tree in the gully.
The grey beach pebbles crack to my boot —
the black sheep scrunch on the tarred weed
thrown by the summer-worn sea.
Where the burn and the wave meet
the water is old-blood muddied
as if some murder had left its stain
and the Atlantic wave chokes
way back in its throat
then spews the mottled phlegm
on the slab of sand.

The tight undercut elbows of the cove
cannot be scaled.
The only way out
is by the burn's steep banks,
what the sheep snack and snack on.

Offshore Eilean Nan Ron guards the strath
but the fugitive wind sheers round
and fists the hill.
The island's ruins lit in the sunset
hold the story — how the last boat
had to tarry for the last hen
the one that skittered under the wharf
and the man refused to board without it
but still they beat the storm.

On the tenth day the mountains declare themselves.
I drop my eyes
coy and shamed that I doubted them.
A vast horse mushroom springs at my feet.
Otter eagle rainbow and the red rowan
bloom at the neck of the loch
and a man is building cairns on the cliff's lip —
the Atlantic nuzzles below.

Last evening, Montesinho
(North-east Portugal)

We pad lightly up the canyon
past weir and piped waters
chestnuts broom oaks myrtles
I as always cautious about plunges
but the leafage holds.

At the end of the path
a confluence of three streams
a sudden emerald pasture.
Two cowbells clink on their leather
and a farmer's hoe thut-thuts
into the hillside.
Neither he nor the cows lift a head.

Sound of water
bells
the hoe tapping
sound of green
and soft footfall.

I thought,
my father with his peasant heart
would call this heaven.
He'd have struck up talk
with this herdsman
about weather, about growing.

Later I found this was close
to his moment of dying.

Mati

She sang out her husband's curses
the morning after the night before
when he'd flung them on the floor —
sang out with her broom
and her mop's hair
till the floor was resplendent
and he slumped behind doors until night,
began the barrage afresh
and in the morning
she buffed the boards again to shining.

She sang to her half-Pekinese
cuddled her aunt, coaxed her to speak
through harelip and missing teeth.
She was brave and rounded —
she dispensed the warm beer
to the men at the bar
kept one eye on the soccer blaring.
She ran the smallest hotel
in the most dried-out village
of the drought, the dam was empty
but her heart brimmed
and her cheeks were polished
with the oil that ran her
that kept her singing.

2

Morning. A welter-skelter of prints
from the night's paws and snouts,
scrunched fern, a loop of intestines
from the fox's rout. Foam-white splatter
of droppings, could be gull, but it's owl
that dark eye, claw and swipe
and there, a fur tail –
what the owl couldn't swallow.
I heard his bark at midnight before he feasted,
and there's his first course spat out
bursting with beetle backs.

5

The trees at dusk tell me *KEEP OUT.*
Secret business. Rustle rustle bump
the witchery has begun, the circles.
How delicious to be excluded
to feel the tremble of the unwanted.

The night's heart thumps and even the moon
is squeamish. Fungus upon fungus deforms
in the dark and the ground heaves with skirmishes
won, unwon, scurrying, scurrying, that nightly chant.

Each night everything is rewritten
and I hurry in the morning to decipher
who went where, what burrow shook
who held the party, but the trees are once again
inscrutable, won't tell who danced
who stripped a bark skirt – if it was fun or pain.

from **Mothering words**

1

At the end of a life
your hands flap about
radar-sweeping the bench
for that lost thing — what was it?
Out of your life's ritual
the one remembered trade —
dishwashing wife.
Is this where a woman ends?
Taking out the plug, putting it in.
Tidying, tidying the dregs.
Your hands hovering like helicopters
above the yellow laminex
the whirr of them scattering objects
cups, forks
jangling spoons.
This here, that here
put away, put away
everything put away.
Why?
You who never cared for the tidy.

2

Daily you pronounce you are lost
all at sea
but you seem to be riding the swell.
Your face shows none of the rage
I would have written on it...

how he who was terrified of dying
was given the snap release
and left you the ragged ending.
After the few days of his farewell
the bustle the shock the lull
that comes around death
when everything is caught and stilled
in that spell
you are left with the longing
to be likewise lulled
but getting none of that…
instead the fractious fraying of your cells
and what you always feared
the babble of the body
that makes a private hell
as it shrieks its details of decay
and those of us watching
wish you could ring a bell to join him
and taste yourself that quietness.

4

The eyes that I used to see brimming
never spilling
are dry now, the rims a salmon pink.
At times the first look of the vacant
the one who is vacating
the one heading out to sea.
You said mountains were your realm
yet you swam fearless of the shark,
surfed tossed tumbled, gobbled sand
your hands wanting neither raft

nor board, confident as fins
and the sea in its subtle ways
replenished you.
So might the fish in you
now be hunting the sea.
To replenish.

6

We your daughters fuss around you
attending you each hour of the day —
bored…restless…hungry…tired?
Though tired you've never allowed
and only the clock lets the day fall.
You who always put yourself last —
the smallest piece of tart
forgoing the cream
the second helpings bypassed for the brood —
you who claimed death was a breeze
are clinging right now to every crumb.
You fight for the chocolate biscuit
and the shock of alone
has your voice imperious at 7.30am.
Where is my tea?
It should be here when I wake! ·
You now the infant —
hatched from your life's chrysalis
87 years in the hatching
with an infant's cry
Don't leave me…rock me…stroke me.
As we your children perfect our mothering,
breathless, running with our offerings,

each of us daughters doing it better and best.
(Your son runs his own race.)
Not a moment is left to weigh itself.
But see the tell-tale sign —
how I still count the helpings.

7

Your skin is repainting its canvas
the colours decidedly autumnal —
dabs of charcoal, russet, mauve,
pointillist blots and mounds.
Brown moons.
I dare not touch.
My hands won't forget
how your own hands held back
when I as a child, pristine, unblotched
clamoured for touch.
And here you are
like a toddler with a scraped knee
upending your leg on the table
for the breakfast bandaid, cream.
I jot the dollops of ointment from the tube —
instruct you to work in the balm.
Obedient, you obey.
Do you guess my shrinking?
Slowly slowly I relent —
learn to anoint you.

9

In your twenties
you grabbed the sail's rope,
at seventy the Himalayan cliff.
There had to be some trick of fog
to ease your grip.
Millimetre by millimetre
the mist creeps in your brain.
Out of a lifetime of doing, rarely still,
you learn to simply sit
waiting for the bus to come out of the white.
The unentered realms are entered.
You who spent so little time waiting
learn to wait.
There had to be some subtle
cunning persuasion to force your fist to open,
for you to slip your mooring –
maybe the fog is that blessing.

10

Each game of Scrabble is a new toy.
Always brings an eager flush
as it has all your life
Yes, let's play, such a good game!
Even now, taking out the box,
your brain is its least scrabbled
as if the lattice of the board
right-angled, never curved,
assures a certain, well-read map.
Though at the start you ponder, flustered
Do I have to hang words, on what, where…?
the map suddenly a perilous grid

but with your first hook of a word
you take hold
and swing nimbly from the letters
darting your bird-hand back and forth.
In the month you reach the life-rung 88
I'd put down MACE early in a game
that you began slowly, overloaded with blanks,
then midway I saw a gleam
as you jabbed the letters GRI in front
laughing, immensely chuffed
you could still deliver.
I heard, in last night's game,
you produced JIGGLER from the rank
totally unbidden –
the brain still juggling word-gems
and you glinting in their light.

11

Flowers thrill you. Taking you posies
I choose the hectic purples, pinks
colours you used to scorn
that now entrance you.
Did you bloom as a mother?
Just last week you put it (to another)
you'd been a mother *mothering with gaps*
and I winced at that bell from the past
ached for what can still lurch at us both
from the fog. But today I catch the remnants
of your mothering words as if they were flowers –
Are you warm? Are there towels?
Small matter that once I leave the room
I'm erased.

When I reappear
your glee *Where did you spring from?*
and the fact that mostly you know my name
are petals I gather for a potpourri
for that time when there'll be no mothering words —
when the huge distinction
who is mother, who daughter
has vanished.

12

One year on…
you greet me *How exciting!*
enchanted with my purple shirt
primp the collar with such motherly ease
I am stunned to quiet — that old whine
You never noticed turns to shame.
One year on…what now but more of this
waiting   waiting
as I watch you showing me the way
as a mother should
past the sign on the gate *Beware the bulls!*
the gate you always charged through.
What bulls now but this yoke of time
that you wear lightly — still upright
still charging through
if at this gentler pace.
In a flash I see the links of flesh
in the chain — your body, mine
no matter whose is which.
Time has no clock on its face —
you are teaching me this.

Road

the country heaves off
to distance
only this index finger
road
is proud with pointing

braggart
I hunt my face in you
the stagnant one is spat out
in your gravel-edge spatter
and it's all certain (mostly)
arriving
holding onto your ribbon
blowing somewhere

what's congealed
tooth   fur   paw   innards
sticks to your tongue
tar-baby
is pegged on your line
for the pickings

and my eye peeled forwards
should stop to read what's scrawled
but forgive my speed…

I am going somewhere   that sweetness
I am going somewhere   that fright
I am going somewhere   that sweetness

only you road know the haste
how we pelt to tomorrow
the country sloughed off
beyond the verges

break out road from your moorings
escape   escape your white stitches
your raggedy edges
the straws and sandals
ring-pulls   butts
flung by all of us
with our eyes forwards
forwards

and with me riding on your back
let's shamble away sideways
slinking snakewise
lose me   lose me

I am going somewhere   that sweetness
I am going somewhere   that fright
I am going somewhere   that sweetness

Cutting onion

Why is it this onion
not that one
pulls on the skein of weeping?
Asks the man to weep
once a year
once a year only
and asks the woman
too full of leaking
asks her to weep afresh
for a solid reason –
cutting onion.
The half of it wide-eyed
in your palm
cry if you must   if you must…
its heart wide open.
Who'd guess under that burnished coat
such a white flame
silken
and the slivers of ice melting
as you chop and slice
and those pearls of onion eyes
with their cool gaze
as you weep
as you scoop the whiskers of frosted glass
to be tanned
sizzled scorched
and you watch the tails arch –
scorpions crying *OUCH*
but your weeping is gone.

Today

the sun at its most generous
everything can be itself
the sun not pushy not hard-fingered
not hot-tongued and feverish
not sweaty not searing
not nosey not bullying not flagrant
not piss-taking not piss-drying
not dam-parching not egg-curdling
not puddle-baking not root-cracking
not metal-firing glass-blowing
instead
magnificent
and also meek as monkish
silent
soft-lipped peach-cheeked rosy-tipped
supremely discreet whilst ubiquitous
everyone welcomes
opens their doors and curtains and windows
their verandah drapings
porthole covers and venetian blinds and blinkers
everyone opens their eyes
salutes with dimples
solar panels ecstatically creaking
pine cones popping
sunroofs lifting
today
all the underlayers the washing the bedding
are airing
all can be divulged
no need to whisper.

The sea-maid's tale

2007

your note   kind
thank you

you'll say strange
but that book that day
all the bells it rang
the sea-maid's tale

so long I've known
felt her twine
the mermaid marooned in my skin

in this place
she began to speak
that inconsolable one

**I collided
there's no other word**

the rock was a shock of hard
the sand was a bristling hand

air was blunt with intent
I could not carry it

nothing held me in its arms

you all say water drowns
but I would say

air is the drowning one

you'd say
that's being born

born

none of you remember being born
do you
so how can you speak of it

but from the moment I landed
unwritten on
I watched
and my skin wrote it down

why did I come
because the marigold sun was calling
because my hair began to grow upwards
and the tips tugged at the roots in my scalp
so I followed

let me tell you

did I hear sun shout

What's this!
Moon, what have you landed!
Months you've been teasing me
with cuttlefish
a random skull
fishermen's dregs

and now
you serve me this

this slip of silver
a pale scrawl on the rock
where a crab stalks
sniffing the altar.

What and who is she?
She?
Yes, her hair
breasts.

Lena I'll call her
the name that's bounced in my head
yes
Lena.

then maybe sun peering

Is she silver?
Already she's tarnishing
to pewter…

look at her head
arched back in shock

how the night wave spat her
way beyond the high tide line.

Look at the long silver rudder
ripped off her spine
see her mouth flung wide
spilling a purple ink…

And what's that?
I have to steady my beam…

in the cave of her throat
what is the wound that drips?

Lena —
Oh cruel shame!
What snatched your tongue
through your lips?

Monstrous wound that makes me blink…

and sun grumbling

Look at me
one big mopoke eye
clogged with all that flotsam
slipslop sandals boards and buckets
noodle packets bottles

and now this wastrel
after a day of staring
and all that water eyeballing me back.
I've heard blindness comes that way!

How can I blink
in this cloudless summer
some ointment is missing
the gauze in the air has thinned
and the red rim of my eye
stings.

All those loiterers
clinging to every drop of me

but lately even they've been squirming
covering   hiding

and now this slimy squid of a creature
with her pale green skin…
what is she wanting?

Do I have to show her the scene
show her living?

moon whispering

Oh girl you are lost to me
lost to me

you begged to be flung from my realm
look what it's costing you

your blood was a purple-blue
the blue of a deep-sea grape

but the rule of the earth is red
so now you must spill to be refilled.

what have they done to my body

what have they cut off
my singing is gone
no tune no tune
only the peep of a pipsqueak gull
have I turned bird with this landing

how sharp is sharp

how many knives I've sharpened
with my steps

I remember that first scream in my feet
or the stubs they were then

even sand jabbed its blade
when vertical was new

and I stumbled and dragged
crabbed along

and those other cuts

how it hurt
when air first burnt my throat

a swarm of bee stings
in my gullet

and then like another knife
the glare
sun-stare
stabbing a bloodshot eye

how moonsick I was
for moon's silky look
but moon was gone

except again her whisper

Like a lamb touched by another hand
scorned by the ewe

so now you've been licked by the air
you cannot return to water

you must find your own circuit.

I had not been child here

I knew no childish songs
but sun urged
go on   go on

I couldn't tell the skin I clung in
how to peel its water sheen
but what I found
when air whirled
on my browning ears
that once were green as sea
what I found
was that slowly where I began
the child was also skin
and I began in little words
inside my cheek

in little words I sang
and childish things
came out in beads and bells
and peeps of birds
that hardly had the wing
oh could I learn
that child was out of play
but had the box and not the key
but could unzip the seam
and find that play was in

how I beamed with sunlight
to be so found

**and wind also found me
whistled me on**

*It's wondrous
this earth is worth seeing...*

*right now you'll not follow my language
but I whistle the past
and future
don't fear
I'll be breathing...*

**breathing
what is that**

as I spluttered on the wind's grist
a fist of air in my throat

and then
as wind got the drift
sidled and simpered

*Yes   gently   gently
let forest closet you
teach you to breathe*

*plug into its lung
here
I'll guide you into green...*

is this forest

Welcome
the undersong of birds begins here
the leaf catches her breath
even sun is abashed
polite as a guest
on our tree-top step. . .

breathing
nothing to it
see us trees
feel the pulse in our leaves
our trunks our limbs
it's all secret
but nothing to it
come slide on your knees
under the fern
we'll show you the way
of the earth's lung. . .

'Where are you from?' a leaf
lavish and green as a map, asks me.
I have nothing to say.

remember
I'd not been child here
I knew no forest songs
but there was undercurrent here
I knew in my liquid bones
underleaf   an ocean's pull

and true
sun was filtered to a quiet tone
a soft-speckled eye
almost moon   the bliss of cool
and air a dimpled green

how small and worm I entered earth's lung
and slowly the trees
hauled me to my heels   my tottering stubs
taught me the tricks of the vertical dance
how to stoop and lean from anchored feet
and toss my hair   with my knees stock still

no need to speak
as the undertow of fern and moss
tugged on my limbs

but then the branches bent to ruffle my hair
yanked me to reach   and climb
don't putrefy there

some days

I felt the earth restless
the rocks remembered moving
and trembled
days I couldn't stand for the rocking
even the trees teetered
tilted by the mist
the weight of its glove
days when the air blew me sideways

and sun was cranky

Nervous ninny
Lena how cautious!
You came for the difference —
you came for the marigold of my hair.
Of course you could crawl this journey.
You could blindfold
wrap and succour your elbows with knee pads
limp three-cornered into the world.
Enough of that slouching under fungus!
Its camouflage is kind for only so long
but this is too torpid.
In what leech land have you buried
your bright eye?
I warned you of the anaesthetic
of forest fumes
fermenting moss —
it's time to bubble out
move   move!
Enough of this buried night
and crevices of bark
where the bird barely flits
so damp and drear.
Child, move out
see this torch through the leaves.
Remember
even in the darkest painted shade
who's the brush?
That's me!
Stir your heels.

I blinked

I came because
because
could hardly remember
what marigold
what starfish
I'd pressed to my forehead

and muttered back

sun
stop yanking at me
can't you tell my bell's silent
the birds do my shouting
take their message
stop whipping me with your scorch
your pushing into world
and weather
can't you tell this morning
my bell's too heavy with its metal
there's no ringing

so stop hauling on my vertebrae
like I'm a chain to some well
and you wanting the well's answer

I'm saying nothing

If the Sun & Moon should doubt,
They'd immediately Go out

but take sun from me
and I'm edgy
drooping in my hair and petals
sultry grey and hemmed with tatters

take this day
today hanging no fire
matt as pavement

why did I come here
why did I don a leg or two
and throw my fin to the surf
my heart all dry with what it wants
and shirks

what do I dare this morning
what weed tangles and entwines
looping back and forth
and I want forth
but the weed turns
and barks
this way dark and witchy

and eggs of chance
crack
and where's the force
to move the timid knee
and push the heel to mount
the mountain here
call it life

**living
is this it**

is this what I landed for

this shriek of my hair
how it snags
and screams at the roots
as if a toddler's pulling it
innocent with a fist
that pulls harder the more I yell
you're hurting
hurting me   let go

is this the world
its crib with bars and poles
and me being landed
now torn
wanting dry land
yet to be let off the hook
to find again my silver skin

as if air is a wave
and it buffets like surf
with its own sting of dust
my fate
to have no bark on my toe
no mouthguard
no guarding dog to clutch

the world began to pinprick me

and people threw their darts
of rictus grins and words that said
another thing from what was spilt

my toes deciphered
what they smelt in the underfelt
but how many years it took
for my feet's speech
to reach my throat

so I heard the world

and sidled onto chairs
my tailbone nudged the weft of cane
and wood
I perched
and no one could decide
if I was dumb
or shy or out of range

peep peep was all my tongue could tweep

I watch their faces

and each year prints its book
but I never see the ink
nor the printer

I watch how the weather shapes the face
rain pocks   wind
and the year's hooves gallop over

face   round like a medal on a pole
round with the open mouth
startled OH   or lean   equine
with the year's hard hooves galloping over

at what hour did the boy's chin
wobble out of boyhood
who remembers cheeks pale pink and apple
the lips hardly stitched
now a capillary scribble
the eye scared to look

face that looks out   one that looks in
eyes with a plastic film   eyes sharp as a trowel
eyes with a possum's gleam
eyes with a trout's stare   eyes bleared by screen

and look at that man for one
with a vertical seam from eye to chin
what's drawn   he stumbles out a reason
how sleep etches a creek line
the dream furrows
and the year's hooves gallop over

but sun comes in again

Watching
watching sends you blind.
If you knew how my eye stings…

watching is a lonely place

let me in you bodies
through the crackle of your coats

one day surely
one day in this circus
I'll find a body
comes from elsewhere
not just a missing part
like my own
but a body strange as strange
a feather on the knee
or a bell inside the shoulder blade
that clangs with a laugh
so far not one's made me gasp

I hear the birds unravelling their speech

chortles grunts and hoots
and then the wings follow
but my own garble stays
just a titter on the bracken floor
and what else can I do
but keep my mouth all sealed

how I wish
I could learn a note or two
and force the song from a stub of a tongue
an old old place
the forge of that
but the fire's not lit

I stand marooned

to travel in this muscle
bone
is a riddle
I can't find the key to fit

scurrying

between this place
that

moon
will you whisper
what I need

and what is home

does water ever need to be told
where to run

sun's fingertaps again

You're too jelly   too viscous
too oyster without shell.

Dry yourself on gravel —
grow to be a solid thing
scrape off your watery gloss
sandpaper yourself on the world's grit.

You're monochrome   monotone
a yawn.

Stretch yourself across my palette.
I'll hand you the brush
paint yourself afresh

scarlet   maroon   copper-gold

imagine desert
vermilion dirt
your last drop of spittle
your last liquid darkening
gone gibberish.

Grow there
grow there from the gibber.

That country's like you Lena
dumb
dust in its throat

so the birds do the shouting.

riddle of empty

this stripping of fur
the moss vanished
spun in a lather of stone

where in this gibber plain
is the dolphin humming

gibber gibber
the women mutter underground
but I can't track them

instead
the wind's shunting brown stones
the car chatters
a gibberish of rubber

and no one's listening

this ground
that can't be buttoned up
in glades
or hollows

flattens its back

flattens its back
against the whiplash
of wheels

a faint sun in the early dusk

Moon where are you?
I thought this was your fullfaced night —

yes here you come
you've cut it fine.

Can we speak about this girl?
I fear she's lost.

The brighter I light her path
urge her on
she stumbles like it's pitch.

She's more your kin —
any message you could send her?

I'm hoarse with blaring this and that.

I've tried teasing tempting and taunting
bossing scathing searing
scowling behind cloud
but I've run out…

she's outfoxed me
I admit.

***Sun, haven't you learnt one sprig
of a thing about this girl?***

*When you stare her out
can't you see her shrivel
pretend to faint?*

*Can't you see
you all-seeing oaf
how you've scorched her
blistered
pocked her with moles?*

*Can't you see her skin
tighten with fright?*

*You've stretched her thin
across plains and scree*

*even the dew runs scared
from your eye...*

*let her hide some more in forest green
let mossy mulch soften her feet*

*let her rock in your subtler arts
what you sprinkle through leaves*

*let her soothe her parched throat
with my silver nights*

give her time to mend her timid heart.

'Between this 'yes' and 'no' I've lost my way'

And *no* pulled harder
doused the palette
to monochrome again

this time shades of black
charcoal   soot

so much for sun's vermilion brush
and desert heat
all I heard and saw was *no*

so I hunch in the elbows
of the fern again
in gully gloom
is the worm here too

and if someone tries to prod me out
I growl and spit
don't come too near

yet what tiny cub
trembles in my blood
whimpers   *yes*
please   yes

clematis   footfall of violets
the violet's face upturned

but   *no*

away

what nonsense lurks in the colour black

and sets on shiver
the merest freckle on the arm

take those slugs on the path
that sooty scrum
slug on slug
how each one trails
the glue of its mother
or brother
who knows

think of the crow's beak
glistening
how the scrum would be swallowed
no aftertaste
no question in the crow's beak
which slug hatched from another

what nonsense black strikes
way back in the heart
and sets on shiver

how do I know
what the moon guards
so stern she is
unturning
and her black face
I never face

and what is safe

I grab for air
but I bounce on her hollow arm

thud

and what is safe

the ants track and track

I curl in the spell of their trails
this way that

the boot of someone snaps a twig
a smell of nylon socks

are you okay

I wish my heart could crawl another way

the forest waits

as if I had a question

the wind ceases its begging

the violet's face upturned
as if to answer

but nothing to say

what is there anyway to speak of

sun could barely be seen on a leaf

Lena
what other side of moon
has snared you?

How lost in the shade you are…
the underskirt of a fern
is no roof for you

you in your conundrum
inside-out
you goatfish minus fins.

What dawn stole your silver sheen?

Where's your goatish leap?

climb girl climb

my foot must
ripen
like the goat's

clematis drops its scent
to lure my toe
and in this forest dark
the white petal
gleams
and vines tangle arms
with sun

so how to find the bridge

or the ladder
to give me coloured rungs
and sun stamping on the shine

so my feet can follow

slowly
slowly green was opening its curtain

all the years I've tracked its face
green the fur of the ground

green the caterpillar's belch
the slash of slime on the frog's knee
green that banks the morning's glint

how the leaf paints green yellow and rust
how bracken draws its web of iron
mustard and maroon

how dusk with its moaning crows
paints black into emerald dark
and grass is silver-lipped

it took me years
but I tugged at the curtain
and green slowly answered

and air sent other tunes

one day
mid-afternoon
the ribbons on a manna gum
clicked and clattered
my eye sprang out to look
and track the sound
and later in the misty dusk
the lyrebird clacked his castanets
my ear stretched out

and this time sun
had nothing to do with it

a jingle came to my lips

I envy the wind
its dry face
how its eyes can peer
in windows
and not smear the glass

I envy the wind
its swirling skirt
how it leaps
and keeps its fingers
free from dirt

how it leaves so little trace
beyond the blown leaf

and wind breathes through me

air doesn't burn

she's had her say
it seems
that wily watery one
marooned in my skin

now perhaps she'll settle down

tell them thanks
I'd best be wandering on
so long

from

married to this ground

2014

as lichen
embroiders the face of granite

as lichen
seduces the fallen log

as lichen
rings the stem of the rose

as lichen
caresses the knot in the bark

as lichen
paints the fence-post orange

as lichen
flowers boldly in the mist

so we are married to this ground

Country life

It's raining. Instantly the lichen sleeves
on the blackwood branches are swelling,
their pale mint-green luminescent in the gloom
while the mistletoe beards higher up in the ribbon gums
have darkened, sodden, and I'm noticing how brown
the ornamental pear leaves are before they drop.
You're replenishing the wood basket
having sawn and split logs in the rain,
rain-froth in your hair, chin bristles glinting wet
your wet-weather gear swishing as you bend
and now the never-fail generator falters, clunks quiet.
Last night the solar batteries hit danger zone
so you're muttering, swearing, and I'm offering
what about the oil? and you heave at the metal frame,
peer at the dip stick, *she's fine!*
Give it a rest I suggest, *sometimes helps.*
You're surprisingly indulgent. *Also have to pump
the dam-tank soon,* your tone on neutral.
Country life. The genny is born again at your urging.
Lichen is another miracle.

When did you two meet?

And we'd say aeons back…

maybe I was a blade of grass
and you some flying insect

or centuries ago
you the maid and I the cobbler
hardly! you protest

or in this recent span —
twenty five years now
since you knocked at my door
asking the way
and I laughed
but then you vanished…

so perhaps we truly met
months later
when I waited an hour and a half
in a side portal of St Paul's cathedral —
it was raining lightly.

Finally
breathless from running
you claimed me.

A miracle I was still waiting
anchored to the bluestone wall
its air of sacredness
as if ballast against the future.

Hurrying to the Botanic gardens
the shrubs and grass gleaming wet
we sought out the green wooden shelter

entwining, rampant
we announced ourselves lovers

we met then.

A geography of marriage

This is how I ask:
You are my path, how do I walk you?
Adonis

Standing beside each other
we're like flanking poles in the ground
both of us tall and thin
deep comfort in our looking out together
from the vantage of this piece of earth
our roost on this plateau
trees echoing our shapes behind us.
What are you seeing?

Other times, when we face each other
when my eyes can still be shy
(dare I admit that twenty five years on?)
my chest starts measuring my breath
eyelids counting *blink blink…*
we escape to the nuzzling position
each of us looking beyond, over the shoulder
or nestling somewhere on the other's body
eyes closed.

Writing this is also a holding of breath
what do I say
what can I say
that is not both loving and treacherous?

The vast avenue that the self walks down in marriage
accompanied, plural
and yet mostly singular

but here in our land of raggedness
there are no avenues
there's disorder
the half-cut stump hollowed by termites

random gesticulations of the bracken
a litter of bark strips striated like goanna tails
the young blackwood yellowing, nervous of the winter.

The bird bowl has shifted off centre
but still balances for the birds' light-footed landings.
Would an eagle topple it?

Is this what you see too
this delicious disorder?

Forget order, forget the avenue.

A new year's eve

The day starts grimly with the Visa bill reckoning
and I start prickling at the sour taint
how your tone takes on that tone
and has me edgy. My mother's cheek would turn
so early on I vowed I'd face any man face on.

The day's heat mounts along with my fuming
and mid-afternoon neither heat abating
I leap in the dam wanting innocence and childhood,
the nicer bits, perhaps a fresh baptism.
Launch the lilo across waterlilies into clear water.

My arching back tweaks and my arm on its overarm
downward scoop snares on slimy weed,
the impenetrable dark of a dam's depths.
But the water's bite enlivens me, the adventure
of leaping waterlilies and I'm almost innocent.

You're still smouldering. You phone your father
in his nursing home, remarking how for the first time
in your life you know where he is but now
he's unreachable. Not the best call for New Year's Eve.
You mutter *New Year's Eve's always a let down.*
We are way out of range of fireworks,
the social dazzling kind.

I decide to spend the evening alone, retreat to the studio
with a cherished book on equanimity. To simply pass
the hours, breathe myself cool. Delicious stillness.
Gradually the heat diminishes. I begin to prepare
for the ritual ascending to midnight,
the 108 strikes of the bell.

Suddenly your strong sonorous voice rings out
from the house *I'm going to ring mine too*
and I rejoice. What other man…So you begin
and then I, man and woman in tandem
hustling out demons.

Not hard to stay with the count, to pause
on the tenth *dong*, then ring in unison.
The stars and the dark receive our medley.
At the finish you appear and we're triumphant
the new year rung in resoundingly,
man and woman clanging and now chortling.
This one I'll remember.

The bed

How still it is, moored on its casters,
how inscrutable
>   all the knowledge of its nightly travel
>   wedged in its foam and coils,
>   printed on the sheets, marine-blue
>   or colour of sand

only the bed knows the weft of a couple's dreaming
>   castles, mountains, the sputtering plane,
>   roads that peter into floodlands
>   the revisitations, that room again,
>   two lamb chops in a glass of water

only the bed knows the weft of a couple's sleeping
>   the pact one half of the bed makes
>   with the body above it
>   that perilous waiting for dawn
>   the backdrop of the other's breathing
>   this great battery endlessly replenishing,
>   the crucial terminal where bodies dock
>   and interlock and vanish to oblivion

only the bed knows
>   how each body writes on the other
>   delicate transcriptions in daylight and darkness
>   gasps and giggles of hunger and satiation
>   the tender goodnight and the chilly,
>   all the waves that roll over the bed
>   as if it's a raft…but it's bedrock
>   the underpinning, inscrutable on its casters

only the bed knows the intricate weft of a couple's loving.

Porridge?

Marriage is like porridge you once said.

Was it just the assonance?
Startled, I didn't reach dismay or think to ask
Do you mean lumpy? Claggy?

The daily repetitions steadying lovers
in their fragile vessel — is it an outrigger canoe?
Something essentially primitive
two hulls, a ribbed platform or a net strung between —
an illusion of safety.

Is it that sort of vessel?
A high mast, a makeshift sail
some days bark some days canvas
each hull flanking the other
ancient knowledge in the weathering of winds
the constant fickleness of weather.

Right now we're anchored at the kitchen table.
Our breakfast is, yes, porridge
and on its grey-white lunar surface
gold rivulets of honey are catching the light.

The sea outside is green and brown —
vertical waves of trees, ripples of tussock.
You say this land reverberates around our occupancy.
In the wide space we hear our own rattling of selves
the two of us, the many of us,
wind in the rigging.

what threads around us

a natural weave

the swooping loop of the young goshawk
the new skink scuttling behind the woodbox
a spider randomly squashed

how the huge leaning gum by the gate
saved its plummet for nightfall
the thunderous crash didn't reach us

how the last crevice-skink we loved so well
vanished, three summers
he greeted and peeped with his chocolate nose

feigned the hanging-dead-skink position
in his woodbox crevice
absented himself

you thought it was bark flapping
from the flowerpot on a windy day
and later

his carcass wedged there in the drainage hole
how many hours to desiccate in the sun

life and death is a grave matter

from **my space**

unnamed

my tiny writing house
poised here on the high slope
free of the shackles of naming

      cypress boards   five cheeks of glass
      five paces across   two steps up
      a sense of aloft
      eight pine legs that never tremble

          *

in here

unseen
my head swivels like a bird's

ur-sounds of creatures
I hear the bat before it flits

skitter skitter in the ceiling
arpeggio of antechinus patter

out there   *thump thump grunt*
the drum-beat of roos boxing
thump grunt

under the rusty mantle of last year's bracken
an almost-rustling that could be blue-tongue

or autumn snake unwinding
shedding the frost from his muscle

Grebe

...here was something more than a bird-call...here was
a secret message, calling...for translation and understanding.
Alas, I...still am as helpless to translate it or to understand it...

Aldo Leopold

On the spring breeze
the flavour of wattle
and intermittent grebe chitter.

Fast loud high metallic chittering
the bird book claims   *vibrating not trilling*
and across the grassy span to their watery theatre
it's this vibration that makes me quiver.

The call not always metallic or nervous,
it can be a light chain running out fast from its spool
or the chink of glasses on a tray
a bossy staccato   or the gentlest chiding.

A fox barks!
how the twilight rattles
fox has the scent of grebe in his nostrils
hear the urgent shrilling

and in the new morning when the dam is again
a stage shining with possibilities
steam rising from its apron,
there's a desolate absence, no *chitter chitter* chatter.
Is that a feather floating?

Then…*teet teet   I'm here I'm here!*
that delicate announcement
and she glides out
her breeding plumage backlit by the sun
fluffed like a tiny feather bed
inviting her lover
and I cheer
my applause ripples on the water

and there they are
the grebes taking their bows
duck-diving in a flurry of exuberance
flashing white under-tails, kicking their legs

and now they resume their motionless drifting posture
demure discreet creatures
such a replete contained air, not a titter.

Eastern spinebill

Such a dapper acrobat!
His black purposive cap
the elongated curved beak like a surgical probe
the chestnut cravat low on the crisp white throat
auburn fluff behind the head,
his particular *flop flop* in flight
as if waving little flags or clapping in gloves.

This morning one full-pelted into glass
splayed himself comatose
allowed himself a minute only
before the vigilance resumed
head revolving wildly, mouth agape
the first flap-flurry but one wing wouldn't follow

and I began plotting how to release him
from his flightlessness
throw a blanket, dash a rock on the fluttering,
bracing for my first killing of the wounded wild.

Would he make it? Would his wing reconstellate
remember flying, flipping and jerking
propelling his deft little body further?

Yes! The tiny heart won out.
He lurched to the mint-bush nearby
perching there half an hour in unlikely cogitation

to let his ruffled cravat settle perhaps
or to ponder that high-wire act
he'd just pulled off, dodging death

and then off he flew
free as a bird.

What bird am I?

I lean to the gang-gang
with her marbled breast and charcoal coif
independent enough
to be on a separate branch
and when her male calls for reassurance
she's in no hurry to placate
but in her own gentle time
mutters soothingly *cool it cool it*
not going not going
and then there's an equable
almost canoodling conversation
from their separate branches
I like that intimate positioning

whereas the grey currawong
another contender
I've never seen as a pair
so her solitary stance is accentuated
and on the days I want that
then I'll give her prime position
for her intensely reflective air
her restful alertness
the calm rotation of her soft grey head
her ground stealth, poise
the days I long for that
I'll say I am her.

from **moments**

last night's sunset   wildly exuberant
        seemed a presage of drought

                    beneath the crimson extravagance was a strip
of the palest aqua   colour of ice
            reminding me of Shostakovich   the tone of the viola
                    how it speaks of the Russian winter   ice

            looking at it you knew there'd be no cloud
for days   perhaps never   that all the bragging was
            happening now in this flamboyance

                    speaking too clearly of drought

                                *

bat-squeaks in the ceiling

in the distance the weighty drone of a tractor
        slashing paths
                    clickshots of stones and sticks

how that tractor plunders the new morning
        the world runs on this   not the bat peeps
                    runs on this weightier growl of engine

                                *

the sea is a long way out of hearing
        but sometimes there's a tang of salt in the mist
            and those high notes in the canopy
                    could be gulls

Threading guitar

The surprise that his hands are those
of a blind man seeing from his fingertips.
No longer the child's hands whose palms I read,
map of the hand, his lines, mounds of Venus.
Now he needs no map at all
he's utterly found.
I'd thought maybe he was a little lost elsewhere
pitching his voice a long way out of hearing
like some sigh of longing
a faint claw at the air wanting someone to answer
or perhaps no one
but these hands have no doubt
they need no instruction
in this task of stringing guitar.
His hands remind me of birds
his fingers their wings lightly flapping
on the fretboard
a decisive graceful fluttering
as the fingertips tease at a knot, loosening
knowing tension is useless
and tension will yield.
Not really like birds.
His head is looking away
whilst the fingers titillate
and the strings trail and tangle
and somehow when the knot has yielded
the strings connect in the holes
there's a purposive tightening of screws

the guitar resumes its backbone
the fluid strings on the spine become taut
he grins that really it's nothing
this knowledge of his hands
his steady shoulders
the fingers knowing all that is to be known
that's when I saw he was flying.

Smothered by quilts

Mice my sister calls them.
Mice. The hordes of women
mobbing quilt shows round the country.
She means their uniform of short grey hair
their bobbing eagerness.

I enter the hall, that cave of many colours.
A sudden pang of loneliness.
I should be soothed and coddled
in this plethora of fabric
but it's November hardly Newfoundland
and I'm sweating, smothered by the insistent
uprising of quilts on every wall,
the overwhelming neatness of squares and rectangles
meticulously hung as trophies.

A smugness in the air.
That cosiness of sewing circles
woman's lineage of stitch and chat
the feverish stockpiling of thread and silk, snippets of velvet
stitch and chat, stitch and chat.
All that worthiness, the nursing homes the needy
how warmed they all must be, givers and receivers.
How many quilts does the world need?

A tweak of guilt, the treachery. Perhaps it's envy.
I'm a woman chasing words not stitches.
How meagre a word on white paper.
Again I'm lonely. My protest is indefensible.
I slink out the door heavily burdened —
a woman chasing words not stitches.

Re-greeting Australia the motherland

From the eggshell membrane of the plane
that peculiar incubating sojourn with four hundred others
I look through the peephole of a rear window
a moment gifted at dawn above the continent's heartland

and way below there's a huge primeval creature crouching.
In the dawn light its coat is maroon
the colour of placenta
a persistent image of birthing

for this creature is also mother
this motherland I was born to
and my eyes fill on seeing her
as if three months away has been longer, longer
yet how strange she is, like no other.

As the dawn lightens
I see rivers swelling southwards.
In this abundant season
her emptiness is watery, watered.
The great red-brown surface shows ephemeral veins, blueish
and there are pale cream and ochre swathes
of water atop salt, hints of aqua

as if she the mother is wearing a clinging silky garment
but underneath you can still see her bulky body
brown and resolute.
Remember, this is a flying rapture
high above the mud and bulldust
the throat can swell freely, throb in greeting

I know her.

Watching my first rugby union match on TV (World Cup New Zealand 2011)

What I notice:

a dispassionate sociological appraisal is impossible

some of the men's faces look very wobbly when the anthems play

the weight of the anthem is heavier than gym iron

the haka is mighty, wondrous

thighs like massive clay pipes squeezed out from teeny shorts

guernseys crammed with pecs and backs as wide as tables

bull necks are bullish

I'm remembering aged seven Punch & Judy and gobsmacked by the clouting

one player is sporting scarlet boots   why?

the commentator hoots elatedly at nostril spurts

red-splashed wound-proud men are reporting to the blood bin like dutiful schoolboys

the split instant between the hero charging and the hero fallen his knee skewed alarmingly sideways

how the scrum of body chunks on body chunks could be like
a giant crystal

but is more like a slug-pile

the commentator relishes telling us *torn scrotums are the worst*

the grace of a hulk propelled skywards

the brawn-scrabble at mud level

oh the stillness the almost-beauty in the frozen scrum after the
loud shout to quieten   to pause   then the mad ramming frenzy

a large white egg has shot out from the slug-pile's birth canal and
lies unnoticed for a whole two seconds

that egg looks exquisitely lonely and innocent before it is seized

the guy with the ball charges at 8 guys lined up   why?   and gets
slaughtered

how much I don't understand.

from

child in the wings

2019

this morning a blue balloon on the dam's edge

    is this the day childhood beckons?

once in a blue moon a blue moon lands
preens itself in the water
two blue moons on the dam's edge

    come back   come back

whose party is it?
how far has it flown this blue balloon
across forest wilderness, ploughed ground?

    remember ten years old the birthday party
    that wasn't
    the friendless girl with a stamp of polio
    no one came

once in a blue moon a blue moon lands
preens itself in the water

    and childhood beckons
    come back   come back

memory
how it punches through
part of a body neatly boxed away
stored under earth

then suddenly a fist breaks out of its coffin
pierces the long-mouldering compost
pear-tree leaves once orange and yellow

or the days it is softer
a seepage from a waterfall
long stilled and dried
with water traces only

seams in the rock the old fissures
from which memory now seeps
        through the skin

no wonder the Greeks called them rivers

> *remembering and forgetting*

called them

> *Mnemosyne, Lethe*

and the instruction was

> *bathe in each of their waters*
> *drink from them both*

the ancient tutelage

> *drink from them both*

memory's flurries

    Mnemosyne's river
        frothing, glinting

    Lethe slurring
        Lethe's slurry

and the child that pops out
      now and then

          from under the blanket

see that child there on the beach
three years old golden curls little round face
her swimming togs with the bobbly bits
dripping down her front almost to her
    chubby knees

and nothing else exists but the stocking net
she's staring into and its pearly catch
the four jelly blobs squidging there
all wet and glistening in the sun
    see her shining rapture

then the farm without a name
so it borrows the name of its place
Langwarrin
and it comes with 23 acres
a huge patch of thistles
a huge patch of potatoes
paddocks and bracken
a draught horse *Popeye*
a black pony *Tommy*
an unnamed dog
a house like a shack
candles and kero lanterns
a boiler for washing, a wringer
an outdoor loo with spiders
a front orchard
back orchard
and a thousand chickens

a whiff of grieving
because our mother our father
had left their home countries

    a whiff of grieving
    because this is not England not Europe
    because the mountains are not mountains
    because the light is too brazen
    because the wattle is not a primrose
    because the gum trees are not oaks
    because green is grey and mustard yellow
    because the birds are too raucous

a whiff of grieving
because this is not their home country

someone says

> a memory is like a phantom limb
> part of your body once
> that can ache

and sometimes it burns with a strange heat

but still belongs

morning's rush for the train one of us always needs
shouting at and I'm squashed middle back seat and
it's three miles of gravel turning right into the last mile
with the train line parallel on our left the race is on heart's
clutch seeing the engine-smoke just in front or just behind
and how badly I want to be on board on the rails and not
jammed in this metal bubble our father whooping up the
chase the slew and weave and scatter of stones but we're
gaining on the puffing train as we always do and swing
onto the tiny dirt platform how lonely it looks pinched out
of the scrub and sometimes time enough to wave the red
flag that's curled in a tin sleeve on the shed wall and
practise Morse code even though the driver knows of
course day after day and there's George the guard in
his navy cap bending down from his steep iron step
his hand stretched out to pull me up the smallest and
his eye so kind and his grin I can't believe it and I keep
looking at his eye and don't watch the gap so his hand
is extra strong gripping pulling then he jumps out waves
the green flag that has its own sleeve and George has
warmed the metal sleeper things ready for our feet
and I'm in the magic zone of the carriage with its spell of
going somewhere so I can forget all the others to their
windows I'm all alone with my nose on the glass and
straight away I'm on the pony I want so much when I
see those sandy tracks winding off into the bush and
they always disappear round a corner when my pony's
cantering nicely and who knows where I'll get to

it's always someone else's
horse that is
this one unnerves me with his knowing
I'm weightless as a jockey   well I wish
how the horse hates the March fly
I dream and dream the perfect horse
and find him   once   and how I love and love
for a day   then his owner reclaims him
you can tell *she* was born in the saddle
and now I'm on a twitchy sour-faced mare
I wobble   my mother never thought
I needed lessons
I wear my biggest rictus grin and they say
how brave and daring
and race me down the gullies
pony don't roll me in the dam I know you want to
don't step on me kick me buck me trample me
don't scrape me off under that branch
I haven't reached the age of sweating
I ride on fear and it quickens from trot
to canter to gallop
I ride on that sweet sweet scent
of a sweating horse at a canter

Smokey with the iron mouth
the grey that runs away with me
free as a scudding cloud of smoke
we pelt up roads and pound round bends
me on his neck like a dizzy fly
and when he cuts the corners
I swivel on his wither
and he bolts through his home gate
and I'm swinging like a hammock under his neck
bumping against his steaming chest
subside on the dirt like a drop of his sweat
stunned to be still

see how memory scatters its debris
like on that beach the other day
flood-littered with trunks branches
foliage from the she-oaks way up river

their limbs sodden and dark-salted
a savage graffiti on the pale
blank page of the beach

that's what memory can do
even without storm weather
it can flood without warning
flooded by memories

can litter its wreckage
bruising what seemed innocent
innocent as sand

you might say nothing much happened
there was no major incident

but how busy it was

all the nerve-sentries working overtime
attending to the possibilities

    what if   what if   what if

I was as virgin of death as they come

      except when I heard
      the rooster's last scream

and when I saw that sack
being carried to the dam

and what was that hanging in the air
when my father warned

      what if   what if
      what if   what if

what else could it be but death?

memory bubbles

>   our father's special way with roosters
>   crooning and cawing with them
>   till they titter round his boots

   then the days there's the axe
   and the stained wood stump
   the chase the screech of rooster
   fresh blood on the wood
   that sweet-dank smell of wet feathers
   in the kitchen sink

the *tock tock* of the ping pong ball on the ping pong table and the
talk that bounces back and over the net with the white light ball
that's like a tiny planet you can blow around the sky and there's
a laughing lightness to it all

   Point Leo my special birthday beach
   the one tree on the dune we claim our own
   the deep bright eye of the rock pool staring back
   and all its secrets in the depth of it
   anemone, crab, black spiky things, green lace
   and then the long long run along sand
   to the surf and all its dumping thrash and dive
   the rough scrape of sand on your belly
   at the end of a zooming ride

>   an alpine meadow
>   cowbells   gentians
>   gentians blue as gentians
>   *gentians gentians*
>   the words ringing on my tongue
>   like bells

The house for all its walls is like a dream.
French windows have a way of streaming light,
how the brightness mostly makes our faces beam

but things aren't always what they seem.
Sure, I tend to dramatize our plight.
The house for all its walls is like a dream.

I face the wall that's red or black or cream.
Our dinner table places are set tight,
we all have fixed positions in the team.

Don't bother working up a head of steam
about the fact the distant sea is out of sight.
I have to trust the sun will make it seem

a swathe of blue, that special gleam.
Remember, how the sea looks is always right.
Meanwhile the walls no doubt have reams

of stories they could tell. Memory's like a stream
and other days it's like a tangled kite.
The house for all its walls is like a dream,
how the brightness mostly makes our faces beam.

over the road   over the road
head-high bracken and grey sand under

don't go there don't go

howls of spaniels up the hill in their bunker
the house all empty   emptied of dogs

don't go there don't go

watsonia white and pink pushing at the door
now closed

don't go there don't go

that woman whose hair flares red as flame
comes once a week with her bag of bones

don't go there don't go

and there's a hush in the wailing
where has she gone?

Frenchie they call her and the house the land
Frenchie's

don't go there don't go

memory
    itself a sort of
    giddi
        ness
    as if there's
    a cliff
    one's been
    climbing
    and now
    looking back
    and down
    the vertig-
    inous dimension
    dizzy
        ing
    as if there's
    a cliff
    one's been
    climbing
    memory
    itself a sort of
    giddi
        ness
    and now
    looking back
    and
    down
    the cliff
    one's been
    climbing
    diz
        zy
            ing

don't stare too hard at anyone

don't look into their eyes
for more than a second

don't stand too close face to face
in case your eyes lock onto theirs

because

hypnosis is a sin
hypnosis is a sin

that's what the nuns are chanting

hypnosis is a sin

that's what the nuns are chanting

when the nun bends down
in her half-moon bib
not one hair peeping
from that white band on her forehead

when she bends down and says it close
quietly like a threat
her eye glassy behind her glasses
a faint breath of cabbage

when she says it close
    if you doubt you are lost

something sings
    yippee, now I'm found

eleven years old *now I'm found*
let off that jangling chain, belief

chuck that little red book
that keeps hammering
with its nonsense
about sin and all its sizes

now I've arrived in doubt-dom

    welcome, this is home

memory
        hops and flits
        like a plump noisy bird

landing here and there squawking
        that time   that place

see the poop-spatters on that rock
        look at the swollen belly

how does it lift off into flight again
        with that gutful of stories

or is it a flightless bird
        grounded   gut-heavy

just imagining?

we are told to sit frozen
this is Bach this is Beethoven
wait wait

the wind-up gramophone in its magic chest
a wooden box high as my waist

the outstretched arm above the whirling shiny plate
our father's hand steering, lowering the poised
needle and then
                    it jitters
          takes off on its own travels, skids
squawks like a trapped bird

then again the waiting
this is Bach this is Beethoven
coming coming

the nervous needle settling back
on the black disc

and we still strapped to stillness in our seats
dare not shift a knee, a foot

wait wait

and suddenly from the needle's eye
the bird's let out of its bulky cage
unleashed and soaring now

and sings
sings so we can melt

and sometimes we are simply girls

sisters forgetting our numbers
dressmaking round the ping pong table

a scatter of patterns, *Simplicity, Vogue*
tiny-waisted models on the covers swirling skirts

our fingers whooshing the tissue paper maps
with their markings *pin here cut here*

folding, smoothing the fabric over the table
flowers, stripes, checks or a plain deep red

the square slim cake of marking chalk snug
in the fingers, pins in the mouth, mumbles

the one in charge with her sure striding scissors
fantasy of scalloped neckline, flounces

all the cotton reels and their colours, bobbins
the word bobbin has us giggling

the cheery *clop clop* of the sewing machine
needle pricking into the poplin

then *try it on   try it on*
squirms and sniggers, frowns, adjustments

pins and patterns and puffed sleeves
fantasy of silk and lace, décolletage

simply girls

We don't want to let our childhood down
Tua Forsström

jump into memory's waters

stay there a while
and feel the skin swell

stay there too long and the skin will
crinkle like seersucker

stay there longer and the body will bloat
a sort of pickling in the river

They are all our mothers,
those little appletrees
                    Robert Minhinnick

a lullaby of apples, Granny Smith and
Gravenstein, Red Rome and Jonathan
and then the green cookers the nameless
worker drones of apples and it's them
I'm closest to in my bed on the farthest wall
of the house and there's the cherry plum
first its blossom then the little red baubles
of its plums pressing up against the glass
and I'm thrilled I don't share a wall
with our parents' room like my sister does
a foot's width between their three dreaming heads
but she's the one who calls out in the night
there's something under my bed sure there is
yeah sure, there's only the *thump thump*
of a roaming roo and then I hear a possum
bite an apple and hear his greedy rasping sigh
so I tell my sister she's mad and how I'm the one
closer to the creatures but there's solid glass
between me and the wild and hardly wild at that
just unmown grass and the surefooted-tangle
of apple trees so I go back to dreaming with those
green cooking apples unnoticed until my time for
ripening comes, mine and theirs

in the distillery of forgetting
there's a silence

like the inscrutable surface of a lake at noon
a mirror that glares back at the midday sun
revealing nothing

how much is swallowed
and secreted
in the lower levels

but this is not lake country
not even a muddied creek

so let me go back to the bracken there
that hides the pond wedged in the gully

black puddle more like it
that boasts russet algae on its rim

and the bracken rusting over it
like a loyal friend

No, No, go not to Lethe
John Keats

the river that encircles sleep
and someone whispering

slim pickings   your story
hogwash maybe

rub it out to a stain
a stain on the rock
where the water once gushed over

no   no

go not to Lethe

not yet

watching the white

        ping pong ball

pinging back

        and forth

sisters musing

        how we played the game

in childhood

        who played most and least

the ball still pinging back

        and forth

untarnished

        nothing coagulating

on its pure light surface

        its white mini-cosmos

just the breathless

        ball

    scam-

          per-

   ing

      free-

          ly

number 4 won't play horses any more
and she'll rear if you try to saddle her
ride her bareback and she'll buck more

but today this midsummer's day
all that steaming heat has fizzled

hardly a hiss from that past, way back
just this vast wide beach in perfect summer bloom

and once again like innocents
we string out in a line watching the surf

my toes itching with that first ever *ouch* of hot sand
the giggly tickle of the wave's frill

Notes

Our property in the Southern Tablelands of New South Wales adjoining Monga National Park was affected by the vast fires of late December 2019 and the eucalypt forest area particularly, 30 plus hectares, was heavily burnt.

inarticulate speech of the heart...from the Van Morrison album of the same name,1983.

life is suffering...a Buddhist reference. The Pali word *dukkha* can be translated as suffering/pain/unease or unsatisfactoriness.

...that book that day – a reference to Hans Christian Andersen's fairy tale, *The Little Mermaid*. My own work 'The sea-maid's tale', a 57 page sequence, was included in *Goatfish* (2007). This work, an imaginal inhabitation of a mermaid's passage onto land, was first stimulated by my seeing the Mermaid of Zennor carving in St Senara's church, Cornwall.

Where are you from?...from 'The Hunter in the Forest', Pablo Neruda, translated by Ben Belitt, in *Pablo Neruda – A New Decade (Poems: 1958-1967)*, Grove Press, Inc. New York 1969, p.227.

If the Sun & Moon should doubt...from *Auguries of Innocence*, William Blake.

Between this 'yes' and 'no' I've lost my way...from *Conference of the Birds*, Farid Ud-Din Attar translated by Afkham Darabandi and Dick Davis, Penguin Books, 1984, p.200.

here was something more... from Aldo Leopold, *A Sand County Almanac*, Oxford University Press 1949, p.159.

*This is how I ask…*from 'Singular in a Plural Form', Adonis, translated from the Arabic by Khaled Mattawa in *Selected Poems*, Yale University Press 2010, p.172.

*life and death…*from the 'Evening Message' in the Zen Buddhist sutras.

In Greek mythology *Mnemosyne*, the personification of memory, was characterised as a river and also a goddess (mother of the nine Muses). *Lethe* was one of the five rivers of Hades and those who drank from it experienced complete forgetfulness. *Lethe* was also the name of the Greek spirit of forgetfulness and oblivion (from various sources).

*We don't want to…*Tua Forsström, *One Evening in October I Rowed out on a Lake,* translated by David McDuff, Bloodaxe Books Ltd, 2015, p.61.

*They are all our mothers…*from 'The Fairground Scholar', Robert Minhinnick, *King Driftwood,* Carcanet, 2008.

*No, No, go not to Lethe…*from 'Ode on Melancholy', John Keats.

Acknowledgements

Various of these poems have been published over the years in literary journals and anthologies.

My special thanks to Ralph Wessman at Walleah Press for his generosity and patience and for his long commitment to poetry. And to my poet partner Harry Laing for his editing help and his great support in living with the work.

www.ingramcontent.com/pod-product-compliance
Lightning Source LLC
Chambersburg PA
CBHW060557190726
48283CB00003B/1044